Dedicated to Niki, Dimitris, L
Dedicated to my wonderfully patien
Dora and her family, our par

Copyright © 2020 Elisavet Arkolaki, Charikleia Arkolaki

Translated into Simplified & Traditional Chinese by Ying Luo.
All rights reserved.

No part of this work may be reproduced, stored in a retrieval system, or submitted in any form or by any means, electronic, mechanical, photocopying, recording or otherwise, without the prior written permission of the publisher, except in the case of brief quotations embodied in critical reviews and certain other non-commercial uses permitted by copyright law. This book may not be lent, resold, hired out or otherwise disposed of by way of trade in any form of binding or cover other than that in which it is published, without the prior written consent of the publisher. Custom editions can be created for special purposes.

For permission requests and supplementary teaching material, please write to the publisher at liza@maltamum.com www.maltamum.com

ISBN 9798485998608

Today, I felt like painting the sea. We took our brushes, watercolors, art pads, and a glass of water and sat on the veranda to paint. A little blue, a little yellow, a little brown and look, that's how it all started.

今天，我忽然想画大海。我们拿出画笔、水彩、画板和一杯水，坐在阳台上开始画画。一点点蓝色，一点点黄色，一点点棕色，看，这幅画就这么开始了。

今天，我忽然想畫大海。我們拿出畫筆、水彩、畫板和一杯水，坐在陽臺上開始畫畫。一點點藍色，一點點黃色，一點點棕色，看，這幅畫就這麼開始了。

I was reminded of the summer vacations we took, to the place where my mother grew up, and I added some rocks to the landscape. Purple for sparse clouds and this green for the hill seem to be a great match.

我想起曾经的那些暑假，我们一起去我妈妈长大的地方。于是我给画里的风景又加了一些石头，稀疏的云彩是紫色的，小小的山丘是绿色的，一切都那么和谐。

我想起曾經的那些暑假，我們一起去我媽媽長大的地方。於是我給畫裏的風景又加了一些石頭，稀疏的雲彩是紫色的，小小的山丘是綠色的，一切都那麼和諧。

We'd go to the beach every morning and play there for hours. All the colors of summer were imprinted on our swimsuits. Intense yellow, intense blue, and intense orange.

每天早上，我们都会去海边玩上几个小时。我将夏天所有的颜色都用在了我们的泳衣上，浓烈的黄、浓烈的蓝和浓烈的橙。

每天早上，我們都會去海邊玩上幾個小時。我將夏天所有的顏色都用在了我們的泳衣上，濃烈的黃、濃烈的藍和濃烈的橙。

I also remembered the small church. It was on the hill. Our grandmother would sometimes take us there before we returned home for lunch. I'll mix a little brown, a little yellow, and a little green.

我还记得那坐落在山上的小教堂。外婆有时会在回家吃午饭前带着我们到那里。我用了一点棕色、一点黄色和一点绿色混合在一起画了下来。

我還記得那坐落在山上的小教堂。外婆有時會在回家吃午飯前帶著我們到那裏。我用了一點棕色、一點黃色和一點綠色混合在一起畫了下來。

On the way back we often picked wildflowers to arrange them in a vase. I think orange, purple and green are very suitable here.

在回家的路上，我们会采下野花，回家插在花瓶里。我觉得橙色、紫色和绿色用在这里再合适不过了。

在回家的路上，我們會採下野花，回家插在花瓶裏。我覺得橙色、紫色和綠色用在這裏再合適不過了。

When we got home, and after we had eaten our food, she offered us the most delicious fruit. Green for the fig, orange for the apricot, and red for the peach.

当我们回家吃完饭后，外婆会给我们吃最好吃的水果。绿色的无花果、橙色的杏子、红色的桃子。

當我們回家吃完飯後，外婆會給我們吃最好吃的水果。綠色的無花果，橙色的杏子，紅色的桃子。

Grandma also had a cat. We played so many different games inside and outside, running after her in the narrow dead-end street. It was, indeed, Happiness Street! Her colors were white, brown, and bright green.

外婆还养了一只猫。我们在屋内屋外跟她玩各种游戏，在一条没有出口的窄街上追着她跑来跑去。对于我们来说，那可真是一条幸福街啊！那只猫的颜色，是白色、棕色和亮绿色的。

外婆還養了一隻貓。我們在屋內屋外跟她玩各種遊戲，在一條沒有出口的窄街上追著她跑來跑去。對於我們來說，那可真是一條幸福街啊！那隻貓的顏色，是白色、棕色和亮綠色的。

In the afternoons we used to take a stroll down the beach again. I'll mix brown, green, and white for the trail.

午后，我们常散步走下沙滩。我用棕色、绿色和白色画出这条小道。

午後，我們常散步走下沙灘。我用棕色、綠色和白色畫出這條小道。

How beautiful those sunsets were!
We take a whole trip back in time
with a little purple, yellow, and brown.

夕阳多美啊！画里的那一点点紫色、
黄色和棕色，让我们仿佛回到了那个
傍晚。

夕陽多美啊！畫裏的那一點點紫色、
黃色和棕色，讓我們仿佛回到了那個
傍晚。

We'd bring our food with us, lay the mat down on the sand and eat under the starry sky. Dark yellow, dark blue, and a dash of red, and we're there again.

我们带了食物，于是在沙滩上铺**开**垫子，在星空下野餐。暗**黄**色、暗蓝色，和一点点的红色，我们仿佛又回到了那一刻。

我們帶了食物，於是在沙灘上鋪開墊子，在星空下野餐。暗黃色，暗藍色，和一點點的紅色，我們仿佛又回到了那一刻。

I remember the landscape changed dramatically when autumn came. We knew then that it was time to leave.
Mom was coming.
The colors are getting really dark now, intense blue, deep green.

我记得，当秋天到来的时候，风景就都变了。那时候，我们就知道要离开了，因为妈妈要来接我们了。颜色渐渐变得暗沉，深蓝，深绿。

我記得，當秋天到來的時候，風景就都變了。那時候，我們就知道要離開了，因為媽媽要來接我們了。顏色漸漸變得暗沉，深藍，深綠。

But look at the composition, how it changes again, and how the hazy colors are making room for other happier ones. Mom also brought along with her white, pink, and gold, and a promise that yes, we would leave, but we would come back again.

但看看这幅作品，看它如何又一次发生了变化，看模糊的颜色如何让位给了明快的色调。妈妈的到来带来了白色、粉色和金色，因为她带来了承诺。虽然这一次她将带着孩子们一起离去，但她承诺，她们总有一天会再回来。

但看看這幅作品，看它如何又一次發生了變化，看模糊的顏色如何讓位給了明快的色調。媽媽的到來帶來了白色、粉色和金色，還有一個承諾：雖然現在不得不說一聲再見，但我們總是還會歸來。

Dear Child,

Every summer has a story. This is a story inspired by my own childhood, and my sister's watercolors. Ask an adult to help you write down the words and draw the images of your own summer story, and send me an email at liza@maltamum.com I promise, I'll write back to you.

Dear Grown-up,

If you feel this book adds value to children's lives, please leave an honest review on Amazon or Goodreads. A shout-out on social media and a tag #HappinessStreet would also be nothing short of amazing. Your review will help others discover the book and encourage me to keep on writing. Visit eepurl.com/dvnij9 for free activities, printables and more.

Forever grateful, thank you!

All my best,
Elisavet Arkolaki

Made in the USA
Las Vegas, NV
23 May 2024

90243344R00019